REALIZATION POINT

Also by Chris Hoffman:

Cairns (poetry)

The Hoop and the Tree (psychology/spirituality/native wisdom)

REALIZATION POINT

CHRIS HOFFMAN

POETIC MATRIX PRESS

Cover image ICE and FROZEN SAND
photograph © by Christopher Brown,

Chris Brown has been photographing the American
West for over 40 years. As a mountain guide, sea
kayaker and Grand Canyon boatman he has spent most
of his life hiking, paddling and rowing to remote places,
and has photographed things very few people ever see.
He makes prints and teaches photography in his studio
in Boulder Colorado. His book of photographs and
essays: *PATH of BEAUTY: Photographic Adventures in
the Grand Canyon*, was published by St. Martin's Press.
ICE and FROZEN SAND exemplifies Chris's belief that
photography is the exploration of the familiar, in search
of the mysterious. www.ChrisBrownPhotography.com

Poetic Matrix Press
www.poeticmatrix.com
www.poeticmatrixpress.com

ACKNOWLEDGEMENTS

The author gratefully acknowledges the following publications in which some poems in this volume first appeared or are scheduled to appear: *Avocet* ("In this Cold"); *The Chrysalis Reader* ("Oasis" and "What We Do in This World"); *Primary Point* ("North Crestone Lake" and "The Man and the Woman in the Floorboards of the Zendo"); *Wild Apples* ("Weminuche Wilderness"); *Witches & Pagans* ("Finally" and "At the Hut in the Wilderness"). An earlier version of "Morning, River Camp" was published in *Cairns* (Orchard House Press / Windstorm Creative, 2005). Some poems in this volume originally appeared in the following chapbooks published by Yare Press: *Songs from Dream Canyon* (1985); *Map & Compass Work of the Spirit* (1987); *Humming to Lizards, Listening to Trees* (1990). Walt Whitman's words quoted in "Meditation at Seaside Heights" are from his *Specimen Days*. Deep gratitude to my friends and family, especially to my wife Susan, our son Benjamin, and our friend Steve Jones. Many thanks to Jim Best for technical support and friendship. And for inspiration, thanks to lineage uncles Walt Whitman and Will Shakespeare and fellow wanderers Basho and Issa.

CONTENT

REALIZATION POINT

FOR MOM

Louise Williams Hoffman, January 1923 – July 2009

From your lips to my ears
came words filled with beauty.

From your hands to mine
came gifts for my life.

From your heart to my heart
came love unextinguishable.

You gave me a model
of woman, of wife.

Now you are changed
to spirit invisible.

Wherever you are
you'll bloom there, I know.

You shine in the hearts
of all who have met you.

And our love travels with you
wherever you go.

REALIZATION POINT

INTRODUCTION

The traditional times and places for poetry include: late at night around a campfire, or deep in a ceremony of remembering our connection with the divine, or at some significant event in our human lives.

Sometimes we need to make a leap to get there.

There are four directions on this earth: north, south, east, west, and the direction we are traveling in now…

REALIZATION POINT

PINES

Pines bristle with it.
Stones endure with it.
I come to the foothills meadow
to sit with it.
For here is another sight
that so fits the tumblers of the heart
that it unlocks the binding bands.

Enormous slabs of rock lean skyward
trimmed with Douglas-fir and ponderosa
just behind the trees that rim this meadow—
a tufted pelt of grasses—tawny, russet, green.
And over all of this and through the blue sky
the sun pours out its syrups of light.

We know that each of us
is but a story that tells itself
within the play of eros and hunger.
But at certain moments
we call good or true or beautiful,
as on a morning in a foothills meadow,
the story stops. The way reveals itself.
And, more intimate than breathing,
we fall inward toward the arms of grace.

TEARS, BE THE NURSE OF HEALING

The metaphors of seed and flower,
of this world and the next,
can't stop me from missing you.

I know every contour
of the emptiness inside;
and it has your shape.

What can I do
but give in to this mystery?
O tears, be the nurse of healing.
Good friends, be my blanket of rest.

Since you have gone,
how wide now I spread
the soft wings of my heart

that in opening like this
I might touch you somehow.

RIO GRANDE

The young big river in the mountains,
its water dark in early morning, cool
and fresh, edged with spruce and alder, glistens
as it eases to the sea.

Over polished rocks, around the scattered boulders,
glossy ripple patterns stand and waver—
the river's fingerprint of water
with its lavish lulling wash of sound.

A hummingbird trills in and hovers—
its gazing eyeball looms as big as a globe—
then zooms away to pinprick, gone.
The river's ripple patterns stand and waver,
now made of newer water.

Seeing and being seen we meet
as we are flowing. Sheets of empty space
folded by mysterious hands become
the river, spruce and alder, hummingbird and you and me,
all meeting on our wandering to the sea.

But follow the gaze inward.
When we sit down quietly, like offerings
set down around the white shell bowl
within the heart—perhaps a feather,
a piece of chocolate, a teardrop, and a prayer—
the bowl brims with clear water
the way the sounding hole of a guitar
brims with music, making us whole.

9

NORTH CRESTONE LAKE
(Sangre de Cristos, Colorado)

Feet that have walked here
before your feet,
created this trail. Other lives
have followed this thread of dust and stones
switchbacking up through Douglas-fir and aspen,
have crossed chattering streams on worn logs,
felt the alpine meadow expand
like a deep breath,
climbed scree slope and snowfield
to gaze down on this lake, held
like a chip of rainbow
in an upturned palm, with fingers of peaks
brushing the sky around.

For a moment your mind stops
while what is here before your mind
continues. Now the shape of this place
lives within you, as it lives
in others who have been here.
When you meet another being,
this place in you can bow
to this place in them.

10

MORNING, RIVER CAMP

(Desolation and Gray Canyons, Green River)

It is early yet—the hour of the gray dawn.
All night we have slept on the smooth thigh of the sand.
Our first waking breath is of air scrubbed
clean by sage and sun, tamarisks and swift water.
Just upstream, the rapids
are still scouring the silence. The river
continues its long, gathering slide.

In the gray dawn the river is dull
as are the canyon walls, while the high gap
of sky floods with luminous blue.
A bird proclaims himself; and then another.
Rising sunlight slants slowly down cliffs
of ancient lake bed sediment, kindling colors on its way—
tawny rock with horizontal bands of reddish brown,
then talus slopes verdigris with sagebrush,
tufted with juniper green. The river's ripples
play with light now, pushing polished patches
of blue sky, roan cliff, and green-leafed cottonwood.

What a good thing it is to wake every day,
and how soon our minds are ordinarily clouded.
Here, like brother canyon wren and sister whipsnake,
we always awaken to the first day. This earth
opens the shutters of our inner house
so the one who is always present
can flow through us into the world.

11

REMEMBER

Not the memories themselves
but the one who remembers—
the beekeeper
of the hive of memory
with its combs of golden sweetness—
the one who stands inside you
as the hours and days flow past,
who has made you royal
by moving your hand to give,
who is utterly unfindable
but always present, truer to you
than the thought "I am",
who companions you around the fire
and is the fire itself.

PARIA CANYON SUITE
(pah-REE-ah)

Named Pahreah from a Paiute word
meaning "muddy water,"
but it starts with none—
just a broad sandy wash in brilliant sun
between banks of packed sand
while sloping just enough
to be a watercourse in runoff time.
Supporting heavy backpacks
our boots make dimples in hot sand.

Low walls of sandstone slowly
shoulder in and rise until
the watercourse is deeper than is wide,
then deeper still—
dry sand and small cobbles,
level, wall to wall,
floor becoming moist, then damp—
meandering bends
and isolated pools of muddy water.
A side canyon enters with a trickle:
Buckskin Gulch.

Upstream by a bend or two
it widens just enough to hold
a camp-sized beach
and some boxelder trees
blazing green against the red of sandstone
streaked with curtain falls of desert varnish
and rising sheerly till the eyes are zenithed.

A pair of raucous ravens
critiques our presence,
their cries echoing
up and down the canyon.

Quiet now and late at night
under the milky stars
lying in our sleeping bags and held
by the hug of gravity,
we look up past silhouetted canyon rims
to see the far reach of everything else,
everything else.

An intestinal labyrinth is Buckskin Gulch,
ten-plus miles of fissure in the rock
by flash flood slurry scooped and scoured.
To hikers here below in twisting narrows,
the light seeps down
illuminating rosy purple amber niches,
alveoli of light, and fleshy folds.
In wider gaps, it spears down straight
on desiccated fox bones on the sand
or bits of rabbit fur or boulders
fallen or a feather gifted
from a red-tailed hawk.

At Raven Camp again.
Strangely, hiking the canyon's
plicatures and folds
un-complicates the mind
and hints at the implicate order.

Further down Paria
the muddy water begins a steady flow—
to stride over as a rivulet,
to pick a way across on rocks and sandbars,
to splash across when all else fails,
eventually to join with it
and slosh on downstream with abandon
as the trail itself dips in and out.

Twelve hundred feet on either side
the sandstone rises
with shell-shaped alcoves at the river bends
big enough for human settlement.
The rock is red, the sand white,
the sky blue, and at the river's edge
life's humming engines of green—
sedges, rushes, horsetail, coyote willow,
and higher up
the lacy viridian whisks of snakeweed.

Four colors.
The cross at the center of the universe
lives within each human heart
moving through the wilderness.

Big Spring is a seep that dribbles sweet
and fast enough
to fill a water bottle quickly.
Maidenhair fern reminds us
of life's doorway.
Pebbles glisten black, tawny, cream
under clear ripples.

On downstream a million toad eggs
have swollen to black commas
of tadpoles that wriggle away
from advancing boot steps.
Occasionally a toad itself, thumb-sized,
hops out of blending with the sand.

At Cottonwood Camp
desert collared lizards
scurry on the ropy bark, halt,
jack themselves up, down, up.

At night, looking deeply
into the clear stream of space,
we step across the bright pebbles of the stars.
Everything now is close to the bone.
Given plant and animal relatives,
given air, water, a chance for fire,
and all the various rock forms of this earth,
how do we craft a life of what is good—
kindness, beauty, generosity,
food, clothing, shelter, and fulfillment—
before we lie down again
and rejoin ancestral dust?

If you find this, peck its pattern
into stone so we can always
remember.

May earth befriend
our sons and daughters.

16

Down canyon again,
thumb on the map
as on a string of prayer beads.
Textures of rock, the clean
scent of desert, the reds the greens,
wet feet, dry air, muscles working,
feet finding balance,
the crunch of sand.
Some pools among the rocks
are big as bathtubs.
On standing after soaking
the air is deliciously cold.

Another word for caution
is quicksand.

At Swallow Camp
a flight of violet-green swallows
shoots like shuttles
up and down the river corridor
threading a deft pattern
of hunting and dining at speed
so fast you can hear them
rubbing the air.

The longer in this place
the fewer words are needed.
Perhaps some day
we will become so porous
the wind will blow through us.

Each of us follows
the spiral of life's path
to the unique door
each of us hopes to enter.

For now, though, our trail leaves the river
crossing flats of arrowweed
and big sagebrush
with the canyon widening
and rising in the distance,
the trail becoming gravel road
that reaches an abandoned orchard,
our promised land, our Eden,
with shade, green grass,
and sour half-ripened apricots
that never tasted so delicious.

LA MITAD DEL MUNDO

Follow the corn back to the field,
back to the furrow turned by the plow.
Follow the honey back to the flower.
Follow the milk back to the cow.

The sweetness of milk is the sweetness of grasses
where the light of the sun weds the waters of earth
while the wind and the bees sing their songs of fertility
for each kind of plant to produce its own worth.

The potato the melon the squash and the bush bean,
the kapok, banana, bamboo and the rest—
each holds in its core a dot of the sun
enwombed by the beautiful woman who's dressed

in a gown clear as rainwater,
who dances by spinning through the blackness of space.
And the dot spreads its light across golden syllables
where the holy encoding of life has been traced.

Now burgeoning forth comes the whole fragile miracle.
With roots in the dirt comes this Eden of green
and in shimmering oceans the plankton and fishes,
and all pulsing food webs with all of their beings.

And for those who have eyes that are able to see it
shine the fibers of energy linking all things

19

like a basket that's woven of fronds from a rainbow,
connecting our essences in a mesh of bright beams.

On your path you may meet someone coming from elsewhere.
Slow down, take your time, to learn who thus comes.
Your connection with life lies within each encounter.
Let it help you to find your own dot of the sun

and its golden rays playing on your deep hieroglyphics
of love and of beauty. Learn to decode them,
and in them discover your urge to create,
your urge for thanksgiving. Follow this urge then

back to its music. Let us be dancing,
letting our footbeats tell the mother we share
we are here and are happy, thanks to her bounty.
So may we be worthy of all placed in our care.

SAN MIGUEL

What we see here is an adobe church—
small, the color of freshly baked bread, of tanned skin.
Buttresses of rough stones slant out
at the sides and corners,
the adobe on them stopping well off the ground
like sleeves of flesh rolled up from the bones.

At the west end,
above the door, there is a squat tower for the bell
with openings for sound,
black rectangles punched out of the sunglare—
the source of that sense of being watched.

The inner rafters, door, and lintel—some centuries ago
this wood was bright and butter-colored,
now darkened like a blood stain.
There is more than history here.
The colonizing Spaniards
threw a Christian cloak around a shrine
that had blessed the first people with visions and
          understanding.

That shrine is still here.
It gives a palpable freshness to the cloak.
See how rich the colors are;
this coolness is more than the shade of cottonwoods.

21

The church takes root here
like a great stone head set upon the ground
that lets you know
you are standing upon her body.

Dominguez Wilderness

A faint trail threads upward
from the river into this red rock canyon
weaving around gravity's jumble
of fallen cliff face. A few bright wisps
of clouds accent the sky's utter blue.

Playing in its bed for eons
the little creek has gouged gorges
and scooped the rock in lazy sensuous waves.
At night the moon's light
gleams on the polish of its living ripples.

The trail leads on into the deep interior.
And where we've never been
keeps beckoning.
No telling when we'll pass this way again.
And in any case, we would be older.

How much the expanse of the outer world
expands the inner. The more and more we look,
the more and more we see there is to see.
The more and more we see
the more we understand
and understand the limits of our understanding.

Today we see the details of the tougher rocks
capping eroded pillars of stone

and the burgeoning green of the fertile horsetail
and new green needles on the piñon pine
and what is being carved in us
as life flows through.

FOR SUSAN

As they walked
he took her hand in his.
And he felt that both their hands
lay on the tiller of the boat
that was their love together.
How beautiful the sails looked now,
and how strong they would be
through any storm.

IF I COULD SAY

If I could say something
to encourage you to seek your heart's desire,
I would say that when we leave here
we come to a shore
carrying nothing but a small pouch.
And our fare, to book a passage
to the other shore,
is to tell the ferryman the essence
of who we are
by showing him the contents of that pouch.

Surely we show a seashell,
for we are beings of water.
And we carry a stone of the earth for its weight
and beauty and because sorrow
is the ballast of life,
and because through this our sheath
of skin and flesh made of earth
the impulse of eternity
reaches out to feel the fabric of time.
We offer a piece of birch bark
or sweetgrass or other incense
for its fragrance
and for the sweetness of the air we breathe,
and a piece of amber, or a candle,
or some other token of the inner fire.

But none of these will matter
unless they have been received as gifts.

For the fair winds that will wing this boat
to the other shore are nothing but
the fond recollections and songs and prayers
from those we have left behind.
Any harm we've created
will cause storms that delay the passage.

The other contents of that pouch
are symbolic twins of every gift we've ever given,
such as sitting with a friend in need;
and they come from following the path
of seeking the beloved of the heart
and by being true and steadfast.
The more of these there are, the lighter
and richer the pouch.

We know that enlightened beings everywhere
all return to the source.
This is an image
like a dandelion in its globe of seed.
With a puff of breath
this song is ended.

BEFORE THE TALK
BY THE FAMOUS SPEAKER

Here we all are,
the audience,
chattering and buzzing
with each other,
waving our antennae
in a friendly manner,
touching mandibles,
displaying iridescent or protective coloration,
emitting eager pheromones,
reestablishing ourselves
in the hive, the swarm, the heap
that is our community.
When the speaker arrives
half of her work
has already been accomplished.

DO IT SLOWLY

Slowly peel away the thick glossy
clothing of an orange.
Fragrant oils spurt like skyrockets
and lubricate your fingers.
Freed of its bindings,
the orange opens a dark hole
where all the tender mounds have pressed together.
As your lascivious tongue begins to water,
plunge your thumbs in deeply,
pull apart the halves of cloven gold.
Separate the juicy pillows, and offer each
as a sweet simile to your lover's lips.

NIGHT HAS SETTLED INTO CAMP NOW

Firelight flickers on the juniper tree.
Sweet smoke rises to the sky.
The stars spread out, abundant
as all the choices in life.
Remarkably, choice by choice,
my darling and I have arrived
at this place and now.

The night is so still
the only sound is the gentle lapping
of the flames. Thinking back
on the long trail, I remember
the knob of juniper polished smooth
by every hand that held there for balance.
I remember squeezing through cracks
and following cairns across slickrock with my son.

Who knows what happens next?
There will be partings, for certain.
I look at the juniper, its shaggy trunk
half dead, thriving, beaten down, contorted
like a hand grasping for light.
Its resinous bitter blue berries
are tiny planets of hope. It persists
as green as my love for this life.

LONG CANYON

The path leads upward
among the tribe of trees.
The muscles in your body
move your carefully articulated bones,
carrying your flesh into the cool shade
where these trees have been growing
since before you were born.

Lean your trunk against a tree.
Most here will outlive you.
Feel its body subtly stretching with the wind.
As your mind adjusts to tree time
you see how every place is different
from every other: *this* root, *this* rock,
this patch of old snow with this lace of fallen needles.

And in certain special places, like this one,
something else is happening too.
It's as though you are entering
a sand painting as the part of the design
that had been missing.
So when your muscles carry you away
a larger design lives inside you
as a gift of this place.

—for Steve Jones

On the Way to Dead Moose Cove
(Southeast Alaska)

Along the long sea passage
dappled dark and shining
the lush green cloak of the rainforest
lies in rumpled heaps and hollows
on mainland and archipelago.

Deep within this weaving
of feathery hemlock, sharp spruce,
and alder bowers, a small bush
is ripening a blueberry—
like a bright bead
at the center of the universe.

Take that berry between your teeth.
Taste the bitter, tart, and sweet,
and swallow. Now
whole kingdoms
surround that blueberry in you—
those throngs of stately trees, the muskeg spongy,
the streams where spawning salmon slap the water,
fjords where glaciers thunder
bergs as big as barns into the sea.

Your place in this web
quickens within you.

The forest spirit,
alert to you digesting that berry

stirs in his cloak
and wonders
what use you will make of this gift.

The forest spirit says:
The place from which you see the beauty
of my life-and-death struggling
is who you are.

A DRAGONFLY

body splotched with black on green
alights, of all places,
on the back of my hand.

The twin helmets of his eyes sparkle
with green needles of light,
his abdomen cantilevers
as a pure curve of grace,
and each delicately wired wing
shines with flakes like mica.

We hold still while the earth turns.

When he flies off
I am more here
than when he landed.

LE CONTE GLACIER CAMP

(Southeast Alaska)

Between the ebb and flooding of the tide
the icebergs stranded on the mudflats wait
like giant chessmen, weirdly shaped,
arrayed, like us, beneath the hand of fate.
In this light they glow electric blue
and melt on mats of caramel-colored rockweed
in slow clear drips. We watch them melt.
And as we watch them we are melting too.
Each shape unique as personality,
from the ever-giving glacier up the bay,
like those we've loved they pause with us a while
then drift downstream to melt and join the sea.
We leave tomorrow on the rising tide.
See how an eagle climbs the empty sky.

BUTTERFLIES OF LONG CANYON

Start with the hand.
Touch the platform that we take for granted.
Finger the granules of quartz,

the glints of mica, in the moist
and fragrant decomposing leaf litter.
Imagine within the soil the white

threads of fungi and thick nourishing rhizomes,
and the earth churners at their work.
Imagine the seeds and spores and pupae each awaiting
        its moment,

and the pirouettes of ions and microbes
around every single root hair of every sun drinker.
Look around in the realm of sun drinkers

at their mass and variety, and think
of all the nectar drinkers, seed eaters, and green stuff eaters
and the eaters of nectar drinkers, seed eaters, and green
        stuff eaters,

and the eaters of their waste and the eaters of the dead
        and rotting,
each with their courtship and mating,
their eggs, their litters, their varied movements and
        migrations,

each life with its own arc of hunger and fulfillment,
and, all of us, passengers on the same wheel of time.
This cosmos emerges constantly like music

whose architecture is carved with detail at every scale.
The surround shimmers with so many invitations
we can accept only a few—

a glimpse of a spangled Fritillary,
a black and orange Checkerspot
resting on its host plant,

a lemon Tiger Swallowtail, each of us flitting
through each other's story
and into our interwoven future.

WINTER SOLSTICE 2007

Dirty sun-clawed snow,
wind bitten,
beside the icy trail.
Looming cottonwoods expose
their intricate neurons of twigs.
One, two, three coyotes
dash across the frozen pond.
A downy woodpecker dissects
his chosen patch of bark.
A small group of humans
gathers at the far side
of the footbridge,
here at the hinge of the year,
as the sun rises,
amazingly,
again—a gold coin
pulled, like the rest of us,
from the primary pocket.

IN THIS COLD

the snow creaks like old leather.
The ski trail slips between trees
and slants up the valley side,
meaning a nice run coming down.
Pine boughs sparkle with cushions of snow.
The pillowed ice-capped stream
reveals in black gaps its flowing secret.
How unfathomable to stand
here, as the trees do,
through all the winter's nights
or through its trunk-cracking storms.
And how copious
the receptivity of this land
to hold our life water in its bosom.
No wonder that after a foray here
we return peeled and clean
as a bleached bone.

FINALLY

When we close our eyes
we entrust ourselves to the buoyancy
of unknown waters,
and we leave with nothing
but the practiced habits of the heart.

In the outer world we practice
in the costumes of our roles
with the tools of our trades
and all our many strategies
for pleasure, power, profit, or prestige.

But each of us is like a flame
inside a lamp. Our
colored lenses of different hues and shapes,
glass chimneys sooty or clean,
make us shine in different ways.
Sometimes when two lamps meet
the flames in each recognize
each other as the same light.

So do we practice being a lamp
or giving light?

When we close our eyes
each of us is but a candle
with its soft blade of flame
set adrift
in a tiny paper boat
on the vast sea of light.

40

SPRING BREAK

Every journey undertaken
with a wondering mind
is a pilgrimage;
and every pilgrimage
is like eating an artichoke:
Step by step we taste each petal
of the mandala flower.
Each is savory
but not the heart of the matter
and so we simplify,
let go.

We may meet
a thousand different ways
of being in this world—
the one family who
through four generations
has run the roadside restaurant;
the two wild men who shave their heads
in the campground restroom
and leave a mess; the retired couple
oblivious to the full moon rising,
canned up in their motor home
watching TV, their generator racketing
through the night; the woman
who arranges cheap ceramic mermaid figurines
along the windowsills of her ramshackle
mining camp house and makes it beautiful
because her dreams insisted.

41

Each of these is a prickly husk
or a sweet fruit around its own seed.
Of some you can ask
"Have you found the key yet?"
Others are too distracted
even to realize they are looking.
We wish them well on their own pilgrimages, help
if we can, as we simplify,
let go, and move toward the center.

Somewhere near the dry plains of mesquite,
tucked in a fold of buff stone mountain
where hummingbirds and cardinals
visit the old peach orchard
is a white yurt
where we sit in simple meditation
and for a moment
the artichoke's thorny heart
reveals itself, and inside that—
a pilot light, a tiny everlasting flame,
that later we carry
into a wilderness of saguaro
and copious wildflowers.

SAGUARO CACTUS

Prickly accordion of water
playing water's music through the dry season,
crowned with white-petaled,
yellow-cupped flowers,
arms raised. Is this music's exaltation
or a blessing for your guests,
gila woodpecker, elf owl—
as your roots reach and reach
touching other roots
and forming the Sonoran desert's
neural network.

WITH YOUR MIND'S EYE

With your mind's eye
you may see it:
a small hut lost in a remote valley
beneath stupendous ice-fanged peaks.
Within the hut: a vertical cylinder
as tall as a person, painted the blue
of high-elevation skies,
with scarlet ornamentation
and sacred syllables laid on in golden script.

Around and around its wooden axle
the cylinder slowly rumbles
powered by a treadle wheel
and making after every revolution
a little brass bell ding.

Invisibly it broadcasts
all of life's polarities:
male energy from one side,
female energy from the other—
yang vibrations, yin vibrations—
making life move on.

And sitting there faithfully
working the treadle day and night:
your inner monk, your inner nun.

IF THE INVISIBLE WERE VISIBLE

My blue jeans would show their half acre
of blossoming fields of cotton under the bright sun,

would show the sweat of laborers, the steaming vats of dye,
the intricate machinery for spinning and weaving,

the hauling by trucks powered with diesel;
my shoes would show the tapping of rubber trees

and would bellow and moo like their leather's former owners
in the stockyards; my house would whisper

in the wind remembering its natal forests,
would show the clay pits and ovens of its bricks,

the excavations for gypsum and gravel,
the mines and smelters and extruders

for its wires; the heated house would swim with pale specters
of archaeoplankton as the gas flame burns them up,

my electric lights, at least seventy percent of them,
would claw the tops off mountains and poison several streams

to get at the black graves of prehistoric forests,
though some would catch the wind in spinning sails

and a few would translate packets of sunlight into current.
Some of my food would gully and salinate the soil

and abuse some distant migrant workers, though most,
I hope, would feed the soil, making bees and local farmers
          happy.

My car would trail a long umbilicus
to deep sea platforms and steaming miles of ruined

tar sands in pristine boreal forests.
Some bank notes in my wallet would be sponges

soaked in blood or tears, others
full of honest perspiration. The net

that holds us extends so far and is so fine
there is no end to it.

WHERE THE BEE KNEELS TO PRAY

Where the bee kneels to pray
and where she eagerly presses
with blind greed as of fire
and the need of water for low places,
the bee is priestess of the colors of light.
She feasts at the bell of the trumpet of seeds.
And her sweet and holy meal
frees the hands of a swirling cross
which scatters pleasingly into the world
abundance out of nothing at all.

HANDIES PEAK

When the whole mountain
lies under your feet,
put there with leg muscle
and deep breathing,
you begin to see
what the mountain sees—
distances expanding
through the polished air,
the steep falling away
from this high reach
of rock and talus with its scabs
of orange and gray-green lichen,
the trickles of sky water from snowfields
and, far down, the brief summer flourish
of alpine meadows, and farther yet
and wide away rolling on and on
the velvet blanket of the forest
to a narrow yellow band of lowland
curving at the horizon.

Like a cone of seeds,
under one of those numberless trees
lies your bundle of daily cares,
whereabouts unknown.

You see daylight and drifting cloud shadows
play across the undulant land
like a blessing
for the largeness of life
and a tap on the shoulder
for the shortness of days.

TRUE MUSIC

These jewel cases of maple and spruce
cradling their carvings of night
and brimming with resonant emptiness,
these jewel cases fitted with humble strings
that are pressed and worried by fingertip and bow,
and these flaring tubes of polished brass
that transfigure exhaled breath,
and these slips of cane, cut away
from the pond's edge, that cry out
when strapped to lengths of wooden pipe,
and the singing pipes themselves
of pearwood, granadilla, or ebony,
and these animal skins stretched taut
on barrels and kettles
where they are pounded and tapped,
and the human voice so rooted in the heart,
all meet in true music as curling wavelets of sound
that lap reassuringly against your shore.

These lapping wavelets are set in motion
by the hand of one who loves you
from the temple at the center of your inner ocean.

WHO DOESN'T LOVE THE MOON?

In the blue day sky, poised
like a pale shell washed ashore
from the sea of night,
it companions us
on our day journey,
illuminated as we
are, from another source.

The light that fills our consciousness
and plays across the hills and valleys
of who we think we are
pours in through an aperture of the heart,
while the heart sings its intimate
songs of hope and despair.

Only slip through this gap
to where the self you seek
is the seeking itself,
boiling with light.

For whether we love the moon
sailing through its phases,
or the simple turnings of the earth,
or the souls of fellow creatures,
the clear light of all our loving
flows from this source.

BRIGHT ANGEL TRAIL

Growing smaller and smaller
I hike into the canyon.

In the rising sun
the limestone cliffs
blush like a ripe peach,
while their etched clefts and crevices
still clutch the ink of night.
A spiralling eagle dwindles to a dot,
dissolves to diamond blue sky.
A half a mile below,
the trail's beige thread
splits the verdigris plateau
then plunges to the river.
Far off, the canyon's northern rim
makes hazy grey-blue shapes like teeth
as witnessed by the tongue.

Growing older and older
I hike into the canyon.
My mind chatters,
paying interest on a lot of borrowed trouble.
I have come to burrow into silence,
deeper...
deeper...

At the river
A raven swaggers up and down the beach.
And like a pebble
I lean against the rock
and listen to the river tumble and slide.
It gleams like quicksilver.
And I have been here
for one point seven billion years.

REMEMBER THIS PLACE

Deep in the forest of dreams
stands an old oak with a thick trunk.
Feel along the rough bark for the hidden
silver catch. When the door
springs open, step inside
and close the door behind you.

There is just enough light
to see the stairway spiraling down.
By the time you reach the bottom
you have disrobed yourself of your body
and left it hidden in a safe place.
Now you are your essence—

how you would have yourself seen
if understanding replaced ridicule.
In this form you journey
with a pair of guides who ferry you
along a river that undulates smoothly
through space like a spilled spool of blue ribbon.

When you disembark, a large reindeer
carries you on its back for a long time
or a short time, as swift as the wind,
to a cave glowing with golden light
from a welcoming campfire inside.
and yellow straw on the floor.

In the kettle above the fire
lies a golden key. Remove it
with tongs and let it cool.
Then in the palm of your hand
look through the key into the heart
of the beast who has carried you so far.

The heart is beating steadily
surrounded by a halo of golden flames,
unutterably beautiful—
it is the heart of the universe
beating with the universal heartbeat,
within every creature and thing.

Bow to the four directions;
raise your arms, touch the ground.
Retrace your journey. Re-clothe
yourself with your body. Step outside
through the door in the tree.
Live your life.

PRAYERS
(Bandelier, NM)

That place in the wild
where the paths cross
of people seeking solitude,
there I will meet you.
There where two stone lions—
wild cat, North American—
crouch side by side,
twin mounds of our first gate.
Sun-bleached antlers
wreathe around the lions,
twin black antelope horns at the pivot point.
Let us leave flower petals there,
between those simple paws,
and tie our prayers
to the branches of the living tree.

THE TREE

I am the tree,
The tree so strong.
I am within you
All life long.
Look to the top—
No one can see.
All things abiding,
I am the tree.

Here is the life
That's ever green.
Deep in my roots
I touch the dream.
Around my branches
A crown of light;
The spiral stairway
From day to night.

I am the crossroads
Of East and West.
No one forsaken,
No one the best.
I am within you
Forever still.
Trust in the tree,
All will be well.

HONORED ONE

For this moment I am outside of time,
alone, on the edge of unknowing,
and fearful of touching my night.
I have cast a small circle around me.

I pray of you, come
in your form of Great Medicine Bear,
your fur glossy and black as the darkness of space,
wearing your necklace of stars,
come in your human size and sit with me.

I know you arrive from the council circle
where you sit with Buddha and Lao-tzu and Jesus
and Muhammad and Krishna and Kwan-yin and all the rest.
The fragrance you bring from that silent conversation
fills my lungs with peace.

Be with me now.
Guard my dreams; guide my life.
Enter thoroughly into me and see out with my eyes
that I might wake up right here, right now
and join you on the path of beauty.

A DREAM

After sailing and sailing these many years it has become clear that I've reached the last landfall of my sister in her kayak. I have found the island called "The Eyes" for its appearance low on calm water with its reflection that so resembles a pair of eyes, almond next to almond. Along the journey I have seen the sights described in her fragmentary journal pages that had reached me in stoppered green bottles and the odd pitch-covered chest. It is clear that she made landfall here, but of her fate past that, it can only be surmised that she met it in the cold green sea.

And so now I have returned to find my father himself gone. And his youngest son, whom we both so resembled, a mere babe when I set out, now calls *me* father, yet says I am likely too old to be his, for he says his own father must have been a strapping young man. And so I have helped him construct a boat with which he may go in search of the true father he believes he must find. And somehow in the drafting and measuring, the sawing, planing, the pegging and caulking, we have grown so close that I know my heart should break were he to set out, as though he were my own son.

And of my mother I have had no news; and of the wife I should have had by now I have had no news, because my life has been spent in this other pursuit.

Yet in all it has been a good one, for somehow now I am seeing in it the rounding of the circle, the arc

58

of my own experience from babe to boy to man to elder touching babe. And when the circle has fully come round perhaps I may pass gently through its opening out of this world and into the next.

WHAT WE DO IN THIS WORLD

Everything we do in this world
happens also, in a different way,
somewhere else.

We pick up a pen to write,
and in this other place
a dog cocks its head to listen.

We walk down the street,
and in this other place
trees rustle in the breeze.

When we help a stranger on the bus
somewhere else a beam of light
flashes between two stars.

The empty ache of our yearning
can open rooms within an inn somewhere
to receive new guests.

And when our heart tightens like a fist,
somewhere else a crude boot
crushes the meticulous web of a spider.

When we blend our voices into the nectar of song,
from somewhere else the inner friend comes
to listen; we call this: "gladness."

But have we yet done the work
that allows the governor of that place
to be wise and good?

And what can we possibly do
to prevent a great withering there
or a torrent of blades?

Stir the pot carefully, my friend.
Your stick reaches farther
than you may know.

MY GREAT GRANDFATHER'S CHURCH

As pastor he would always take the calling
from the poorest congregation
because it was the most in need.

Strong beside him,
my great grandmother bore
nine children in twenty years.

Picturing his church so old
I thought of hand-cut stone, brass rings in oaken doors,
huge windows glowing biblically inside.

But I had forgotten the poorest congregation—
in those days German immigrants,
with services in their native German.

So when I found his church today
of course I found it standing in the poorer part of town,
still a church, but always humble,

now well worn, though not quite shabby,
like a family Bible handed
down through generations.

In this part of town the door was locked midweek.
I kept touching the foundation,
wanting to reach through it to him

62

and to my own foundation,
to my father and his father and his,
as I take my son to look at colleges, now
as his foot is on the threshold.

THE DARK CURTAIN

Each time I part this same dark curtain
I enter a world I've never seen before.
One time, the market vendors lure me to a castle
by serving perfumed teas in rooms of taffeta,
and your skin is the temple of spice;
another time I slip through brilliant seas
holding a singing sloop close to the wind,
and you are the speed of it;
or I am a panther
and you are licking my fur;
or I am an orchestra and your music
ravishes me for days and nights on end.
But somehow, blessed be, in every world beyond this curtain
we reach that shining, holy place
where dew touches the petal of the rose.

TENDING THE NEW GARDEN

Weeds come.
Bird poop lies in Buddha's lap.
Deer have nibbled away
all the bright marigold blossoms.
And yet a spider
makes a home among rocks
placed here just last week,
wooly thyme begins to spread
its dusky green,
water rinses Buddha clean,
and with a little plucking
weeds go.

FIREFLIES

On endless summer nights when I was young,
at just child height above the fields of grass
the fairies floated with their glowing fairy lanterns.
We captured constellations of them
in our mason jars and water glasses.
And though we always let them free into the night
the image stayed within
of how we could ourselves be fields of light.
It was only natural to begin
to find our clues through nature
of how to grow up right.
We could be pure as driven snow
and have the lion's courage,
be strong as a gorilla, ox, or bear,
resourceful as a grazer finding forage,
persistent as an ant, industrious as beavers,
own the eloquence of singing birds
and as a fox be clever.

We tadpoles changed into our various frogs,
but now the world itself has changed.
The purity of snow is toxin tarnished,
the oceans emptying of fish, the glaciers in retreat,
the eloquence of birds deserts the spring,
the last gorillas' muscles sold as meat.
And the fireflies, the fireflies, from all our memories fading,
drifting over vanished meadows
over rivers now dammed and piped,

66

into the ghostly forests of trees clear cut
and mountains ravaged—where have they gone?
What will now inspire our fields of light?
In being too many or wanting too much
or squandering what we've been given
we do this damage to ourselves,
this damage to our children.

WEMINUCHE WILDERNESS
(San Juan Mountains, CO)

Freshly squeezed monofilaments of spider silk
link spires of spruce and fir trees
high above the darksome trail, and glisten
in slivered shreds of morning sunlight.
With elevation gained, the trees hunch lower
avoiding the lush and newer green
of avalanche meadows strewn with boulders,
eventually stretching dark green fingers
along the rills, invading swaths of tundra.

High up in couloirs and under cliffs
snowfields like beached clouds
trickle into rivulets that join
like a bird's toes and plunge
through space with rainbows to the creek below
that churns and drops, then slides
as clear as polished air
over chestnut-colored rocks then drops
and pools again and drops.

In the meadows, mountain goats
with puzzled faces have snagged
and combed away their winter wool
on twigs and wands of willow.
The shoulders and thighs of the high tundra
are the old bones of the earth upholstered
with thin cushions of green and jeweler's flowers,

68

some with the scent of healing cleanness.
Here it becomes clear that everything still
is also in motion and changing.
Just as the goats are being goats and browsing,
the tundra is tundra-ing, the boulders bouldering,
the creek is present and is also flowing.
The jagged peaks point beyond the sky.

When the sun is shining
nothing is more beautiful than this.
But when the weather changes
from sunny to sullen in seconds
and thunder bludgeons
the great space embraced by the mountains
we suddenly remember
each heartbeat as a gift
that rises up to us unbidden from the darkness.

WHAT ARE YOU DOING WITH *YOUR* LIFE?
(Lost Creek Wilderness)

Even when the air
seems to hold its breath
clusters of wiggling green dots
bustle about the upper bodies
of the aspen, alchemizing sugars
out of sunfire, air, and water
while the trunks stand serene
sheathed in powdery chamois-smooth bark,
muscular and sensuous as shaved legs under pantyhose.
Where the branches have fallen away
dark eyes keep watch all around.

No More Beliefs

That is what I want:
the deep knowing,
unassailable, imperturbable,
the black rock firm
against the clashing wallop
of storm-seized seas,
the clear flame in the heart,
the intimate whisper
of the one who has unfolded
the map of my life
and loves me yet.

But this I, wanting,
is only the shell of the almond.
The sweet meat within
has already given it all away.
Try capturing five square yards of music
and tacking it to your wall.
Time's silken thread
slips through our fingers.
When we approach the infinite pool of holiness
awe pacifies the tired discursive mind
and we step in and dissolve—
darkness into darkness, light into light.

Thou

All the different aspects of my self
pitch their tents around a central fire,
basking in its play of dancing light
that burns away both hatred and desire.

The fire is known by countless different names
each of which misleads in its own way.
Just as we name sky-falling-water "rain"
but know it not until we've felt its plashes on our skin,
been pelted, misted, smelt it on hot rocks
and caught its melting pellets on our tongues,
just so this fire eludes our every name,
whether "precious seed" or "thousand-petalled flower"
or "friend who fills my heart with healing power
and comes in times of need." And yet
the fire is like a dawn within a dawn.

In all the sad and lovely universe
that lives by eating of itself each day
the one trustworthy point and truest guide
is this flame-like aperture inside
that leads beyond itself to a newer day.
And when my tents have folded, as certainly they will,
just pour my essence through this gap of time
to where the living heart of beauty welcomes all.

AT THE HUT IN THE WILDERNESS

Twin guardians flank the eastern door.
A rainbow, curving, seals up all the rest.
Enter humbly, dropping all you think you are,
and with a heart receptive to be blessed.

Your flesh goes first tonight, and then your bones;
and both are safely set aside.
Your pattern lies inside of these—
the lines intended as your guide.

When these are broken, bent, askew,
or poorly seen, your life goes ill.
But when they weave in beauty
with the greater beauty, all is surely well.

So invoke the hoops of every realm
and every hoop pass through.

O rocks and minerals, water, air,
I am your relative,
so may I treat you well.

O green and growing things,
I am your relative,
so may I treat you well.

O eagle, spider, frog, and all your kin,
I am your relative,
so may I treat you well.

73

All races, genders, tribes of humankind,
I am your relative,
so may I treat you well.

O mystery deep, whose hands have made
and now repair our broken lines,
I am your relative,
so may I treat you well.

Presently, in the vast gap of space
with its blackness and blazes,
there is a vibrating column of air
around which
your body wraps itself. Here
at the lip of the falls,
where the stream of now pours into then,
a bird is singing. How intimately
you know this song! It is
yours to bring forth.

O subtle pattern of our journey,
O lines re-clothed in bones and flesh,
the dawn has come.
May we wake up at every choice
and find our paths fulfilled in beauty.

Summer Shower

Darkening storm clouds
marble the sky.

Leaves tattle
on the breeze.

The first raindrops
stipple the pond.

The bruised, ripe sky
jaggedly splits white.

The whole atmosphere cracks
and the old one crumbles.

Rain raining fresh
sounds its plush patter,

rain raining rain
flooding the gutters.

The last plops
pucker the puddles.

Water drools
from the eaves.

Opening, the rinsed sky
reveals its ribs of colored light.

BLUE BEADS

Days deep into the Grand Canyon,
exploring a side canyon alone far enough
that the big-muscled river behind
was just an anchoring murmur,
I swept level a forearm's breadth of sand,
place four blue beads—
gifts from a friend—
in a diamond shape, sat,
gave thanks, and listened inwardly.

Twenty five years later I still
can't put into words how the unexpected
invisible light funneled down
past sandstone, limestone, shale and schist
to where the green plants and I
sat vulnerable, or how
I may have slipped through that opening
into a different life. I only know
I am still unwinding that thread.

Since the only things we truly own
are what we do, my friend,
whom I never met again outside the canyon,
whose body has returned to dust,
and who, though barely knowing me,
honored my dream of four blue beads,
owned a share of my happiness
then, and owns it now.

—for Wesley Smith

MEDITATION AT SEASIDE HEIGHTS

I grew up with sand between my toes
along the Jersey shore
so I have seen the ocean many times,
but I've let it look at me perhaps just twice:
Once, after staying up all night
to bake my first baguette of bread,
I brought the bread to break it open
crusty and steaming
at sunrise on the empty beach.
More recently with my wife, my sisters
and their spouses, again at sunrise,
the ocean placid, lapping gently, and receptive,
we gave our mother's ashes back
to the waters we had splashed when we were children.

This is the beach Walt Whitman visited
more than a hundred years ago
when he "hardly met or saw a person.
"A broad expanse of view all to myself," he said,
"refreshing, unimpeded—that spread of waves
and gray-white beach, salt, monotonous, senseless,
striking emotional, impalpable depths,
too big for formal handling."

Today, midway in life's journey,
I walk with my old friend along that beach
on the broad herringbone of the boardwalk
thronged with people, some with jiggling
bodies bagged haphazardly in shorts and tee shirts,
others firm and smooth, their sexuality

barely leashed in bonds of shiny lycra,
all moving to the midway music
of bored barkers, the gongs rattles and clangs
of games of chance, the solid roll of steel wheels
of the roller coaster, the tilt-a-whirl,
all of us perspiring freely to the sea breeze
while our tongues caress the sweet nipples
of soft-serve ice cream cones.

"Forget all that nature worshipping crap,"
says my friend. "Real life is here!"
He's right, of course. Everyday mind
is Buddha. We just don't always see it.
Instinctively we're drawn to this margin
of the outward infinite—that spread of waves
and gray-white beach—and then the wide blue sky
fills with airplanes towing advertisements.
Here at this border all the engines of desire
hum and throb their loudest.
And in this family of desire
we are all relatives.

The boardwalk sprouts a curtained booth
for Psychic Readings by Sabrina.
At this border with the inward infinite
the High Priestess and Death and the Magician
waltz through her hands,
but if she's good, her constant messages
will be "Pay attention,"
"Love," and "Don't get distracted."

—for S. L. Paulson

WHAT IS REAL

Perhaps all that is real
is this connection
like a clothesline,
always there,
on which we hang
the clothes of our lives
and forget what is
holding them up
in the breeze and the sun.

KISS

I remember our first long kiss
overtook us beneath that cottonwood
of majestic girth and height.
The teenagers driving by honked
and hollered. The streetlamp
cast its pool of light into the mild evening.

Some say each life is like a thread
from birth to death. But perhaps it's rather
like a mist of water crystallizing
into a snowflake, that kaleidoscopes
through countless shapes until it melts again.

And thus the past is never distant
but rather like the inner core
of the cottonwood that blessed us.

And the pool of light from that first kiss
is still expanding through our days.
I see it shining in your eyes today
and in our son's eyes shining.

A Father's Wish

The hands that changed your diapers,
held your hands steady as you learned to walk,
now help you tie your necktie
for the high school dance.

I wish I could keep you safe forever,
bundle up everything I've ever learned
and give it to you, beyond what I've given,
the way our ancestors bundled a live coal
when moving fire to a new camp.
But that would somehow be
to cheat you of your own life
and, anyhow, impossible.

I can tell you I've learned
the ego is the seedcase of the light.
When you find that place in you
where you and I are one
I may not be here in my body
for you to tell me.
So let me say for my part now
I see your radiance.

And we have moments like this one.
You saw the beauty, wanted
to photograph it, asked me
to take you there: the neighborhood lights
mirrored in the black water of the lake,

full moon, drifting clouds.
Few words needed between us—
when a butterfly from the other world
sipped nectar from my heart
and settled, sheltered, in yours.

HELPING MY SON PACK TO LEAVE

I am proud of who he is.
I make suggestions
but it is his turn now to choose
what he will take or leave behind
because it is his journey now, not mine;
and with luck I will not live
to see his journey's end,
though I hope for many years
of visits, calls and letters on the way.

In any case, the best I have to offer
is invisible and by now already packed,
I hope, deep within his heart
to be there always, taking form
when needed, as those packed sponge pellets
he once had as bathtub toys
expanded and took shape when wet—oh, look:
a dinosaur, from Dad,
with love.

WORDS SAID TO WATER

Patient in glaciers,
impetuous in streams,
flinging yourself off cliffs
into the waiting arms of gravity
while flaunting iridescent scarves of spray,
salted and brawny in the Pacific
or steaming gently in my teacup,
contemplative as clouds, returning as rain,
wherever you pour forth
sweet and clear and flowing
all the other minerals of my body
bow down to you,
o humble sovereign, bride of my thirst.

THE WORLD RENEWAL CEREMONY

starts here.
All the materials
are at hand.
Whatever presents itself
is the work,
and the work is your altar.

Though the mind can explore endlessly
the mazes it constructs,
ultimately the situation resolves
to you alone with the cosmos.

But the cosmos is also
your bone and flesh.
So there is nothing to fear,
only the question: How
do you treat your flesh and bone?
And the question: What power
reaches through you to set it to beauty?
And: How do you step out of the way?

THIS BLISS

You are the banquet of desire
and I would paint your lips with kisses.
When we enfold in love—
four legs, two hearts, one center—
we enter the green of the summer lands
where death cannot bind us
nor old age oppress. Of course
in fluid time our bodies change,
but through the sacred promptings of our flesh
we know the place beyond the reach of longing
where you and I in perfect presence meet
forever. Together joined, we pour
through fur and feather, fin and fern
until we flood the universe with us becoming it,
then step beyond. Though sheathed in flesh,
through you I know this bliss.

Away

Today I am far from my true love
because life leads our footsteps where it will.

O wind whispering in these pines,
you are the same air that right now
touches her ear. Say to her my loving
is as constant and near to her as you are.

Say: I inhale her love with every breath.

NOSTALGIA

There is a place of satisfied desire,
a place for everything you truly are,
where you, without disguises or dissembling,
are exactly who is wanted, needed, there.

We think we should remember where it is
and feel the pangs of sorrow when we can't.
Yet a glimpse of beauty, or a kind wise word
can put us here again right now—planted
where we always are and always are connected.

The mind can cease its seething with opinions.
And our friendship is a promise to each other
to help each other this transition make:
to organize our lives around awareness
as a crystal forms around its seed
or a flower radiates with its corolla,
to sing ourselves assuredly alive
as a bell knows how to sing its proper note
when it is struck awake.

I HAVE SEEN

I have seen the stag
with the moon between his antlers.
But the animals are leaving now.
They are leaving.

I have seen the stag
with the evergreen wreath around his neck
and the ribbons of four colors.
But the animals are leaving.

The white bear's paw scrabbles
for purchase on the melting ice.
Even the running salmon are losing faith
that we humans will keep our covenant.

As the dark larch and spruce trees
touch the stars with their tips
the moon has waxed and waned, waxed and waned
for a thousand thousand years.

But now whole forests of evergreen brown.
The bats' and hummingbirds' sticky tongues,
the bees' pollen-catching legs
arrive too early or too late.

The stag with the moon between his antlers,
the one who speaks for all the animals,
looks deeply into us, then turns away—
perhaps forever.

RARA AVIS

(Costa Rica)

A stream in the rainforest
cuts a canyon through green
where shafts of sunlight
finally touch earth.
Sunlight pours
past the vast leafy vaults of the tall trees—
pillars lifting the sky,
light cascading leaf to leaf
where everything is growing on everything—
five hundred species of tree in this region,
and on them epiphytes, mosses,
liverworts, bromeliads,
and the droopy telephone cables
and thick hawsers of lianas
older than the trees they weigh down,
each tree a garden on one trunk;
clusters of this green and that,
tiny specks of green and leaves the size of platters,
leaves like shields and leaves the shape of daggers,
all heaving upward in a slow wrestling
for sunlight and food—
strangler fig trees enclose and encoffin
the trunks of the trees they grow on;
crumble and rot, half-rotted,
burst into green again;
tree ferns; the air all sweet
and musky, and damp as an armpit;
A quick tanager
flutters a splash of red;
fallen orchids drift on the stream,

90

the stream's clear liquid light under bowed grasses,
green canyon walls of leaves
round green pointed green
ribbed green smooth green
shagged bright and dark—
a green tapestry of shine and shade
subtly rippling on the tall trees.
And through this green gap of light comes flying
a morpho butterfly—
twin palm-of-the-hand-sized flakes of blue sky,
winking,
illuminating for a moment like stained glass
the cathedral dark of the forest.
A green-feathered precious gem
with a clear slippery needle of a tongue
hums and hovers
then zips away.
In the distance a troop of howler monkeys
hoot among themselves.
Rain begins to rattle on the leaves,
and as evening falls there comes
a tropical fruit salad of bird calls,
then the counterpoint of frogs
with their metallic honks and scrapings,
and sounds of insects too—
the high-pitched stinging trill of the cicadas,
the knitting clicks of beetles, and more,
until the whole blind night
becomes a mystic choir
chanting of the beauteous forms
forever pouring out of emptiness.

SPECIFICATIONS

Of course it would have to be compact and portable.
Like a good pocketknife equipped with tools, it would
come in handy in a variety of emergencies large or
small. If you were to open its cover you could admire
its tiny golden gears, its coiled springs and silver ratch-
ets, whirring and clicking. In detail it would be as
delicate as lizard toes; in texture, as fine as mist; in
transformation, as pure as photosynthesis. It would live
in memory as a sweet melody. It would be a few words
sewn carefully together in a sequence magical. When
called to mind or said it would bring you to listening
from the core of your heart to the wisdom in countless
diverse voices, each speaking toward the fire of what is.

MORE PEBBLES

The man and woman pattern
in the floorboards of the zendo—

Had I not been here I never
would have seen them. Now
they show me my mind.

&

After long absence
old friends return—
chokecherry blossoms.

&

The ego—
a necessary eggshell.

But now
your teacher's beak
pecks from outside:
time to hatch!

&

Each rapids on the river—
another silver skull
pinned to the chest.

We call to our deep friend
by one of his or her many names
as the circumference
calls to the circle—
"Reveal yourself through me."

ଔ

Stripping the cucumber
of his handsome green suit—
naked whiteness!

ଔ

The orchestra conductor's jacket
wrinkles and un-wrinkles
in perfect tempo.

ଔ

When I first got here
I jumped up and down on the sidewalk
in front of
The Bureau of Seismic Research.

ଔ

On the mountain—
rain pool
in a dimple of granite

Flowering yucca—
a cascade of bells.

ଔ

The road
from my mouth
curls around the sky.

ଔ

Abandoned
cicada husk—
where do we go?

ଔ

Sensuous clothes
amplify
our nakedness.

ଔ

Old notebooks burning—
the flames leap up
into this poem.

ଔ

Pissing by the trailside
yellow
autumn leaves.

The morning after
a night of spiritual frenzy—

Perhaps this is what it will be like
after we're dead:
Sitting around,
eating breakfast,
discussing the dance.

ᛩ

Watching within,
one might mistake
that someone is watching.

ᛩ

What is the prayer
you most want others
to pray about you?
Say it now
about them.

ᛩ

Shortcut a trail—
scar your own face.

Watching the years pass
with the eyes of a rock,
the trees growing up and dying back
make a brilliant blur.

ॐ

On the trek to Everest
from children's hands—
fresh peapods!

ॐ

As with a mountain,
my losses
are part of my shape.

ॐ

I discover
the sexy young woman
in the photograph
is my great aunt.

ॐ

During the concert
of Indian ragas
everyone was beautiful.

Unscrewing the garden hose,
my hand is jeweled
with water.

಄

Typing a long manuscript
rain
on the window ledge.

಄

Etymology: pry open
the word's pearly shell, behold
its glistening body.

಄

By the bathroom sink—
her red hairbrush
with the rubber band
                on the handle.

಄

Notice:
The surface of this paper
has been carefully treated with ink
to make the words more legible.

98

Ideas—
heat lightning
in the cloudy brain.

⋈

An apple tree in blossom
hums contentedly
with bees.

⋈

The heart-mind
rims a mirror
into which the passing world
glances.

OCTOBER

Soon the spendthrift trees
will scatter the brilliant coinage of autumn.
Today the cottonwood leaves, still yellow-green,
paddle tremulously, and blonde striations of grasses
whisper on the luminous hillsides
where a few dark evergreens
seem to brood on the coming season.

In the meadow where the last
of summer's green has seeped away
hues of claret, roan, and sunset violet
mask the matted gray decay of years gone by.
The sun, our ardent benefactor,
now runs his southern course.
So into the dark we go.

What can be our refuge now,
our place of ease, as fat times fall away?
Not this; not that; only the ah! of compassion,
to remember what our bones know:
that all things hang upon each other;
and, as true acolytes of beauty's way,
to perceive the stillness within all forms,
the Thou arising, mirrored in the heart
of every living being;
and, like those crickets choiring on the hillside,
to sing ourselves toward the unfoldment of time
as out through a blossoming flower;
and to recall, when the green time comes again,
it is always just like this.

100

THE RAVEN'S DAUGHTER

O the moon, she calls to water,
And ships call men to sea;
And I have heard the raven's daughter
Calling, "Lover, come to me."

And I have gone at midnight
Down to the sandy shore
Where the sea winds, salt and rushing,
Brought her cry once more.

Bright notches on the water
Where the moon has chipped the tide—
And I would swim to the raven's daughter
If she would be my bride.

"O let me be your ocean
And kiss your pushy prow
And glide along the sleek of you
And buoyancy endow.

"With wind I'll fluff your creamy sails,
I'll make them yearn and stretch—
Each crescent taut and luminous.
I'll fly you with my touch.

"And I will journey farther
Than any man would go

Because I've heard your singing
Of what my heart would know.

"O daughter of the raven,
Why do you call to me?
For you are Queen of all the night
And I am weak and far at sea.

"The water has turned to blackness
And all my hope is gone;
I fear I've given all my life
To see you on your throne."

"O tiny tiny human,
What foolishness you are
To leave the daughters of the earth
And follow me this far.

"For now your deepest longing
Is dug too deep to fill,
And you must open up your heart
Or else your needy heart you'll kill.

"And you shall open up your heart—
This is my gift to you.
For all who journey with the heart
Become what they pursue.

"Grief," said the raven's daughter,
"There's grief throughout the earth.
The womb of your heart must break her waters
To give you second birth."

102

O the moon, she calls to water,
And ships call men to sea;
And I have heard the raven's daughter
Calling, "Lover, come to me."

And I have gone at midnight
And walked the sandy beach
And raised a ladder to the moon
And it was out of reach.

IN A FOREST OF WESTERN REDCEDAR
(North Cascades)

With three or four friends,
arms spread wide
fingertip to fingertip,
you can just encircle the trunk
of one of these giants.

Thousands of them, standing
as a forest, brood over a world
of shadowless dream light
and hush.
This is because long, long ago,
a box carved of cedar wood
hid within itself all the light of the world;
but now a little leaks out.

In fact, two glints of it
right now are staring at you.
This very bear
owns a cedar box carved
with sleeping under a fallen log
in a rainstorm at night.

You focus and look,
yourself owning a box carved
with learning the letters of the alphabet.

The bear knows the season of thimbleberries
and where to find good buds.

104

You know what you know
but it is very different.

After a deep look
the bear crashes off.
Now inside your own box
you discover something new.

A PERFECT DAY

When the fruit of summer's ripeness
hangs heavy on its stem
climb high to find yourself.

Trace the rushing creek
through somber forest shaggy with lichen
to the clear brown-eyed lake below the divide.

The alpine meadows are turning russet now.
Yet the bell flowers still ring out
their lavender blue, and the sun's warmth
pleases the plump marmot today
on his rock above the willow brake.

With each foothold higher on the earth's back
you step out of yourself
and out of yourself again, unpacking
yourself like a set of Russian dolls
or nested Chinese boxes, until
with the last step out of yourself
everything else steps inside of you;
and you step to the place that's firm
even when this moment powders and blows away.

TANGIBLE MAGIC

In my early days of radio,
vacuum tubes glowed orange and gave off
heat, and reeled in streams of music
from the transparent immaculate air,
delivering me into a new world beyond my town.

Then I used my soldering gun to wire together
rainbow-striped resistors, the disks and lozenges of
       capacitors,
shiny coiled inductors, and the silicon crystals
of tiny diodes and transistors
into magic patterns,
the smoke from the solder's rosin rising like incense.
When I added electricity
these lumps awoke
and siphoned sounds from an invisible world.

Now I try to do the same with words.
While offering incense smoke from pinon or juniper
I solder nouns and adjectives and verbs together—
words like "pumpkin seed"
and "owl's feather" and "amethyst" and "snake"—
using wires of syntax, into magic patterns
to shape a talisman of sound
that comes alive with breath
and connects us with the world invisible.

THIS MOMENT

Somewhere, this very moment, a sea breeze
is making the fronds of palm trees softly clatter.
Out on the reef a small black fish patrols his mound
of brain coral, muscling the water.
In the village a few dogs wander the dusty streets,
painterly dabs of color hang festooned on clotheslines,
charred humps of rubbish smolder, rhododendrons bloom,
wooden dwellings stand on posts.
Shops and houses, some tidy, some slumped,
dress in fresh or faded green, mauve,
pink, sky blue, or yellow. A plastic
bottle lies squashed by the roadside.
Half-finished concrete buildings
sprout bouquets of rebar. Sheets
of corrugated iron slowly rust.
Cheap Chinese backpacks dangle from strings
in the market, next to heaps of onions and beans
and the tooth-white flesh, the dark brown skin
of roots of cassava. Each human being there
moves toward his or her purpose, muscling
the ground under foot, the pencil between the fingers.
Greetings are given and received;
smiles open like slices of papaya.
This very moment someone is happy,
someone is lonely, someone reaches toward a lover,
a child is whimpering, fingers strum guitar strings
while a drum keeps rhythm. A scintilla of light

from the placenta of a star's birth in the ancient reaches
      of time
arrives over the shoulder of the crescent moon
above the palm fronds gently clicking in the breeze,
this very moment.

THE PADDLE

When the paddle slips upward again
after its dip, there remain only ripples
and the forward momentum of the craft.
When a man slips away again
after his life, there remain only ripples
and the momentum of his soul.
What and how do these ripples touch?
That is the question for a man of worth.
He hopes: a wife and child or children nurtured
in their becoming, firm friendships,
ripples blessing the community of beings,
hearts gladdened, the earth herself
in her gown of sky
served as an honored elder,
and the water purer
for the paddle having passed.

OASIS

On this clear night
a small watch fire is flickering
and waving its tendrils of spicy smoke
beside the well in the inner courtyard.

Your host has served you
lamb with pilaf and sweet tea
and now you are alone in the late hours,
within these four sturdy walls,
watching the stars swing imperturbably
as they have for generations.

A meteor strikes like a match across the sky.
From somewhere, muted by the distance,
comes the music of a lute
and the rhythm of hands on a drum skin.

Looking back on the long journey
it seems the days were beaded on a string
that led inevitably here,
though at the time most were just an effort
to discover how to do one's best,
and some just felt like failure.
But now the gems of days stand out.

And now the name of names
forms on your lips,
not to attain or ask for anything,

but simply in gratitude
and to participate in the flowing forth of life;
for nothing is ever completed,
only renewed.

REALIZATION POINT

Deep winter.
Hoar frost graces
the needles of the pines.
The path to Realization Point
is felted with fresh snow.
Yet it's a short walk
and in any season
the view is available to all who look.

Who can deny the pull of the heart's treasure?
We seek it all of our lives.
Desire keeps us leaning into the future.
But our deepest knowing will keep still
to converse with a wise stone
or to consider the lilies of the field.

If I discover enlightenment
will it stay found?
And if I fail, will it be lost forever?
Today the path to Realization Point
is felted with fresh snow.
After our walk
we sip our cups of tea together.
Moment follows moment.
The time and place to live
is now and here.

REALIZATION POINT

AUTHOR BIOGRAPHY

Chris Hoffman is an organizational consultant, ecopsychologist, and poet. He has facilitated human development in a variety of business, educational and therapeutic settings, including 23 years as a senior organization development consultant for a Fortune 500 energy utility company. He currently focuses on organizations working for sustainability. He is a licensed professional counselor. Chris has taught ecopsychology at Naropa University and has delivered many workshops and presentations on applied psychology. He enjoys performing his poetic work both solo and in collaboration with dancers and musicians. The Afro-pop band *Monkey Siren* has recorded his lyrics on two CD's. His wilderness experience includes backpacking, mountaineering, and river-running.   He lives with his wife in Boulder, Colorado. They have a son in college.

 (More information at www.hoopandtree.org)

www.ingramcontent.com/pod-product-compliance
Lightning Source LLC
Chambersburg PA
CBHW030843090426
42737CB00009B/1086